The Greatest Bible Stories Ever Told
Stories that
Build Character

Stephen Elkins
AUTHOR

Tim O'Connor
ILLUSTRATIONS

BROADMAN
&HOLMAN
PUBLISHERS
NASHVILLE, TENNESSEE

A WHALE OF A TALE

Jonah 4:2 You are a gracious and compassionate God, slow to anger and abounding in love.

One day the Lord spoke to Jonah the prophet, "Go to the city of Nineveh and tell them that God has seen their wickedness and they must stop sinning." But Jonah didn't want to go. So he decided to run away from the Lord. He boarded a sailing ship bound for Tarshish.

But the Lord knows where we are every single moment.
He knew Jonah had disobeyed His command, so He sent a
violent storm over the sea.

The wind roared and the waves crashed against the ship.
The sailors were so afraid they began to pray to their false
gods. They even threw the ship's cargo into the sea to make
it float better.

But where was Jonah? He had gone below deck where he lay fast asleep! When the captain found Jonah sleeping, he shouted, "How can you sleep when we are about to be drowned? Get up and pray that your God will save us!"

The other sailors began to think that Jonah was somehow responsible for the storm, so they asked him, "Is it your fault we are in this terrible trouble? Who are you? Where are you from?" Jonah answered, "I am a Hebrew. I worship the Lord of heaven who made the sea."

"What have you done to anger Him?" they asked. "I am running away from the Lord. This storm is my fault," Jonah replied. Suddenly a giant wave crashed onto the deck as the thunder cracked louder! "What can we do to calm the raging sea?" the sailors cried. "Throw me into the sea and it will become calm!" Jonah said.

But the men did not want Jonah to die, so they rowed even harder. But the storm grew wilder. "Forgive us, Lord," the men prayed. Then they picked Jonah up and threw him into the raging sea.

Suddenly, the sea was calm. Everything was still.

When this happened, all of the sailors made promises to serve the God of Jonah. But poor Jonah was sinking deeper and deeper below the waves until a great fish swallowed Jonah whole. There he stayed for three days.

When Jonah realized what had happened, he began to pray. "I am in deep trouble, O Lord, and yet You saved my life. Hear my song of thanksgiving!"

As Jonah continued to pray, the giant fish was swimming toward dry land where it spit Jonah out. The Lord spoke to Jonah for the second time. "Go to Nineveh and proclaim My message of salvation." This time, Jonah went straight to Nineveh!

For three days Jonah told everyone in Nineveh, "Repent, or God will destroy this city in 40 days!" When the people heard Jonah's voice, they knew he was preaching the truth. All of Nineveh believed God and declared a city-wide day of prayer and fasting. They turned from their evil ways and blessed the God of Jonah.

God was pleased with the people of Nineveh. But Jonah did not like these people who were from a different culture than his. They were the very same people who had done terrible things to the Hebrews years before. "This is why I didn't want to obey You," Jonah said to the Lord. "I knew You would bless these people, and I don't want to see them happy!"

"How can you be so selfish?" the Lord said. But Jonah went away to a place outside the city. There, he built a hut and watched what would happen to Nineveh. God caused a huge vine to grow up over the hut to provide shade for Jonah. Jonah was very happy. But then at sunrise, God allowed a worm to destroy the vine. When the scorching hot sun rose in the morning, Jonah was miserable.

Jonah lashed out at God, "It would be better if You just let me die!"

"Do you have the right to be angry about the vine dying?" asked the Lord. "Yes I do," Jonah answered angrily. "I'm so hot!"

"How selfish you are!" said the Lord. "You are more concerned about your own life than you are about the lives of the 120,000 people in Nineveh who need a preacher to teach them." Jonah finally understood the importance of obeying the Lord and sacrificing your own life for the sake of others.

Affirmation: I will obey the Lord!

CHILDREN OF WISDOM

Proverbs 3:5 Trust in the Lord with all your heart.

King Solomon, the son of David, wrote the book of Proverbs to help us live godly lives in an ungodly world. "Wisdom" is the key word in this book. "Having wisdom" means that we live our lives as God would have us live. Wisdom will keep us from making mistakes. Here are some key verses of wisdom from the book of Proverbs:

Trust in the Lord with all your heart and lean not upon your own understanding; in all your ways acknowledge Him and He will direct your path.

The fear and respect of the Lord is the beginning of wisdom.

Respect and fear the Lord and stop doing evil things. This will cause you to be healthier and happier.

If the Lord loves you, He may test you. Do not be angry at the Lord if this happens.

A wise son makes his father glad, but an unwise son causes his mother to be grieved.

Even a child is known by what he does.

Train up a child in the ways of the Lord and when he grows older, he will not depart from them.

Do not withhold correction from a child, for if you discipline him, he will not die.

Be honest with everyone. Tell the truth and do not lie.

Affirmation: I will love and obey my parents!

THE PRODIGAL SON

Luke 15:24 'For this son of mine was dead and is alive again; he was lost and is found.' So they began to celebrate.

Jesus told this parable to His disciples. There once lived a man who had two sons. One day, the younger son came to his father and said, "Father, I would like my share of your property now." For he was to receive half when his father died. His father gave him his share.

The son then took the money and all that he owned and traveled to a faraway country. There, he spent all his money having a good time and doing things his father had taught him not to do.

Then a terrible famine swept across the country and the boy had no money for food. He was very hungry!

To stay alive he took a job feeding pigs. He got so hungry, he would have eaten the pig food if someone had offered it to him. "My father's workers have plenty to eat," he thought. "I'll go back home and say, 'Father, I have disobeyed God and I have disobeyed you. I am not worthy to be called your son. But please, I only ask that you make me one of your workers.'" He left for home with a broken heart.

While the boy was still far from the house, his father saw him coming. His heart was filled with love and mercy. He ran as fast as he could. "My son ... my son has come home!" he shouted.

He threw his arms around the boy and kissed him. "Father, I have disobeyed God and I have disobeyed you. I am no longer worthy to be called your son," said the boy.

But his father replied, "Quickly, bring me our finest robe and put it on my son. Put a ring on his finger and new shoes on his feet. Let us prepare the biggest meal ever and celebrate. For my son who I thought was dead is alive; he was lost, but now is found!"

Meanwhile, the older brother had come in from working in the fields. When he heard the music and dancing he asked, "What's all this celebration?"

A servant replied, "Your brother has come home and your father is preparing a big meal!" This angered the older brother, and he refused to go into the house.

His father came outside and pleaded with him, but his son answered, "For years I have worked for you and done everything you have asked. Yet you never honored me in any way or celebrated my loyalty. But when this son of yours comes home after wasting all that you gave him, you have a celebration. It's not fair!"

"My son," said his father, "you are always with me. I love you and think of you always. Everything that I have is yours. But we must celebrate the homecoming of your brother ... for the son I thought to be dead is alive; he was lost, but now is found!"

This parable taught us that it is never too late to come back to God, for He always loves you!

Affirmation: I will be glad when sinners come to Jesus!

THE BEATITUDES

Matthew 5:3 Blessed are the poor in spirit,
for theirs is the kingdom of heaven.

Jesus began His ministry near the Sea of Galilee. There He
began telling everyone the good news of God's coming
kingdom. He healed every kind of disease and sickness.
The people loved Jesus. Every day the crowds grew bigger
and bigger, so Jesus went up on a mountainside where
there was plenty of room for everyone to gather. There He sat
down and began to teach the people.

"Blessed are the poor in spirit, for theirs is the kingdom of heaven. Blessed are the ones who mourn, for they will be comforted. Blessed are the meek, for they will inherit the earth. Blessed are the pure in heart, for they will see God. Blessed are the peacemakers, for they will be the sons of God."

Jesus went on to say that we are to be happy when people say unkind or untrue things about us. "Rejoice and be happy," He said, "because you will have a great reward one day in the kingdom of heaven."

Affirmation: I will be happy in Jesus!

SALT AND LIGHT

Matthew 5:13a   You are the salt of the earth.

Jesus said that we are the salt of the earth, and real salt always makes people very thirsty. And when you're thirsty, you want a drink of water. Jesus told the people that we're supposed to be very salty and cause people who see us and hear us to want to know more about Jesus; to make them thirsty for God's Word. He said that if we lose our saltiness, we can't make people thirsty.

Jesus also said, "You are the light of the world." When people walk in the light, they can see all the dangerous things that might have hurt them if they stumbled in the darkness. God's Word is like a light. So when we share our light and tell others about Jesus, we brighten their lives. We help them see Satan's stumbling blocks.

But if we hide our lights under a bowl and tell no one that Jesus lives in our hearts, our friends and family may never see Jesus, and fall down in the darkness.

Be a light!

Affirmation: I will be a light!

DO NOT WORRY

Matthew 6:33 But seek first his kingdom and his right-eousness, and all these things will be given to you as well.

"Look at the birds flying through the air," Jesus said. "They do not plant gardens to get food, nor do they pick corn or gather the seeds they eat. Yet, your Heavenly Father feeds them. So do not worry about what you will eat and drink," He said, "for you are much more precious in God's sight than these birds. God will provide what you need."

Jesus went on to say, "And why do you worry about your clothes? Look at the lilies growing wild in the fields. They do not make their own clothing, yet they are dressed as splendidly as a king. Our God has provided clothing for flowers; don't you think He will provide clothing for you? Have faith! Do not worry."

God has given us a promise:
Serve God first and seek
to do the right things, and
He will give to you all
these other things.
That's a promise!

Affirmation: I will serve God first!

27

DO NOT JUDGE OTHERS

Matthew 7:1   "Do not judge, or you too will be judged."

God does not want us to judge another person's actions. That will be His job. Rather, He wants us to be concerned about our own actions. That's why Jesus said, "Do not judge others, or you too will be judged. And in the very same way you judge others, you will be judged."

Each of us has done things that were not pleasing to God. In God's eyes, we are all sinners. Jesus said, "Before you tell your neighbor about a speck of sawdust in his eye, first take the plank out of your own eye. Then you will see things more clearly."

Affirmation: I will not judge others!

WHAT SHOULD WE THINK ABOUT?

Philippians 4:8 Finally brothers, whatever is true, whatever is noble, whatever is right, whatever is pure, whatever is lovely,... think about such (these) things.

Once again Paul dips his pen into the ink and writes another letter. This time he addresses it to the believers in Philippi. "Thank you," he writes, "for all the many ways you have helped the cause of Christ. And be sure of this, that He who began a good work in you will help you to complete it. Our God is faithful. So continue to work without complaining or arguing and live together in peace. That way you will shine like stars in the universe."

"And finally brothers and sisters, whatever is true, whatever is noble, whatever is right, whatever is pure, whatever is lovely, whatever is admirable, think about these things. Practice what you preach and the God of peace will be with you. For this, friends, is the secret to being happy: we can do all things through Christ who strengthens us!"

Affirmation: I can do all things through Christ who strengthens me!

COLLECT ALL 10

Word & Song
AUDIO BOOK

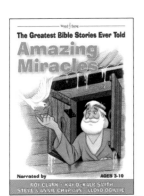
0-8054-2471-7

0-8054-2466-0

0-8054-2470-9

0-8054-2469-5

0-8054-2474-1

0-8054-2468-7

0-8054-2473-3

0-8054-2475-X

0-8054-2472-5

Available in Your Favorite Christian Bookstore.

0-8054-2467-9

We hope you enjoyed this Word & Song Storybook.